No. CX

THE MINOR DRAMA.

LOVE IN '76.

AN

INCIDENT OF THE REVOLUTION.

A COMEDIETTA IN TWO ACTS.

BY OLIVER BUNCE.

WITH CAST OF CHARACTERS, STAGE BUSINESS, COSTUMES, RELATIVE POSITIONS, &c., &c.

AS PERFORMED AT LAURA KEENE'S THEATRE, FEBRUARY 28th, 1857

NEW YORK:
SAMUEL FRENCH & SON,
PUBLISHERS,
38 East 14th St., Union Square.

LONDON:
Samuel French
PUBLISHER,
89 STRAND.

No Plays Exchanged or Sent on Approval.

INTERNATIONAL DESCRIPTIVE CATALOGUE

OF

PLAYS,

AND

DRAMATIC WORKS,

With a Descriptive List of Amateur Plays and Articles.

CONTENTS.

ALL MAILABLE ARTICLES IN THIS CATALOGUE SENT POST FREE.

In ordering and remitting by Mail always send Post Office Orders if possible.

POSTAGE STAMPS TAKEN IN PAYMENT.

NEW YORK:	LONDON:
SAMUEL FRENCH & SON,	SAMUEL FRENCH,
PUBLISHERS,	PUBLISHER,
38 E. 14th St., Union Square.	89, STRAND.

Payment MUST accompany each Order.

A Catalogue with above Contents Sent Free.

☞ Those who receive extra Catalogues, kindly hand them to Friends.

THE MINOR DRAMA.

No. CXI.

LOVE IN '76:

AN

INCIDENT OF THE REVOLUTION.

A

COMEDIETTA,

IN

TWO ACTS.

BY OLIVER BUNCE.

As Performed at Laura Keene's Theatre, New York, Feb. 28, 1857.

TO WHICH ARE ADDED,

A Description of the Costume—Cast of the Characters—Entrances and Exits—Relative Positions of the Performers on the Stage, and the whole of the Stage Business,

NEW-YORK:

SAMUEL FRENCH,

122 NASSAU-STREET.

Cast of the Characters.—(Love in '76

As produced at Laura Keene's Theatre, 28th Feb., 1857.

Mr. Elsworth, - - - - Mr. Stoddart,
Lieut. Harry Elsworth, - - - - - Ringgold,
Capt. Walter Armstrong, - - - - - Lingham,
Major Cleveland, - - - - - - Burnett,
Captain Arbald, - - - - - - - Benson,
Lieutenant Marvin, - - - - - - Hays,
Apollo Metcalf, - - - - - - - Johnston,
John, - - - - - - - - - Harcourt,
Soldiers, - - - - - Messrs. Jackson and Kelleg.
Rose Elsworth, - - - - - - Miss Laura Keene,
Kate Elsworth, - - - - - - - Alleyne,
Bridget, - - - - - - - - Howell,

Period.—*Early part of the Revolution.*

The events of the Comedy occur during an Afternoon and Evening.

Costumes.—(Love in '76.)

MR. ELSWORTH.—Shad-cut brown coat, brown or black breeches, shoe-buckles.

LIEUT. HARRY ELSWORTH.—Red, turned up with blue, buff breeches, high boots.

CAPTAIN ARMSTRONG.—Blue, turned up with buff, white top boots.

MAJOR CLEVELAND.—Red, turned up with white, breeches, high boots.

CAPTAIN ARBALD.—Do. do. do.

LIEUTENANT MARVIN.—Do. do. do.

APOLLO METCALF.—Gray Shad, square-cut suit.

THE LADIES.—The costumes of the period of '76.

STAGE DIRECTIONS.

EXITS AND ENTRANCES.

L. means *First Entrance, Left.* R. *First Entrance, Right.* S. E. L. *Second Entrance, Left.* S. E. R. *Second Entrance, Right.* U. E. L. *Upper Entrance, Left.* U. E. R. *Upper Entrance, Right.* C. *Centre.* L. C. *Left of Centre.* R. C. *Right of Centre.* T. E. L. *Third Entrance, Left.* T. E. R. *Third Entrance, Right.* C. D. *Centre Door.* D. R. *Door Right.* D. L. *Door Left.* U. D. L. *Upper Door, Left.* U. D. R. *Upper Door, Right.*

*** *The Reader is supposed to be on the Stage, facing the Audience.*

LOVE IN '76.

ACT I.

SCENE.—*The drawing-room in the residence of* MR. EDWARD ELSWORTH. *Garden seen through doors.* ROSE ELSWORTH *occupied at a small table, stitching.* KATE ELSWORTH *stretched languidly upon a sofa, with a book in hand.* MR. EDWARD ELSWORTH *in an easy chair, with newspaper in his lap. Writing materials on table,* L.

Kate. Oh, dullness! dullness! I do wish Harry was at home, or Sir William would march some of his troops this way! What's the use of an army in the country, if one can't have a dance once in a while?

Rose. What, indeed! All I desire is, sister, that they should be [*Enter servant with letters for* MR. ELSWORTH.] left to the dance! That much they do very well.

Kate. I'm sure, Rose, I can't see what you find in these rebels to admire. As far as my observation has gone, they are only so many boors. There was Captain Arthur. Was there ever such a dunce? He had no manner whatever. He attempted once to walk a minuet with me, and I really thought he was a bear accidentally stumbled into coat and slippers.

Rose. You're quite right! he never should have got his appointment until he had served a campaign in the drawing-room. If I were the Congress, I'd appoint none who could not bring diplomas from their dancing-masters.

Elsworth. Ha? 'pon my word! Very extraordinary news. [*All coming forward*

Rose. What is it, papa?

Els. There has been a battle.

Rose. Is it possible? Oh, where, sir?

Els. On Long Island. [*Reading.*] Washington has been defeated—has evacuated the city—is retiring northward. [*Speaking.*] I feel, my daughters, that our situation is becoming here unsafe. We shall be continually exposed to the assaults of marauders. It would be wiser in the present aspect of affairs, for us to seek a securer residence in New York, now so fortunately in possession of Sir William Howe

Rose. I should prefer remaining here.

Els. Would it be safe, Rose?

Rose. Yes, for we neutralize each other. Your loyalty will secure you with the tories, and my whiggism will protect us with the other faction.

Els. Your whiggism, Rose. You shock me by such an avowal; and your brother, too, an officer of the king.

Kate. I don't think there is much danger, if Mr. Armstrong is near to protect us.

Els. Mr. Armstrong?

Kate. Oh, yes, papa! He's got to be a captain.

Els. Not a rebel, I trust.

Rose. Not a traitor, I thank Heaven.

Els. You confound terms strangely. A traitor is one false to his king.

Rose. False to his country, sir. A king is a creature of to-day—your country a thing of immortality.

Els. Your king is your sovereign, by divine right and true succession.

Rose. Then, sir, serve the Stuarts. How came the house of Hanover upon the throne? You see, sir, that if you zealous loyalists could shift off James, we, with less belief in the divine right of kings, can shift off George.

Enter MR. APOLLO METCALF, C. D

Met. Good day, Mr. Elsworth. Good day, young ladies. Good day all, I may say.

Els. Have you any news of the war, Mr. Metcalf?

Met. News—plenty of it, and mad. The country is depopulated. There isn't a youth with the first hope of a beard upon his chin, who hasn't gone with young Armstrong, to join the army.

Els. Young Armstrong?

Met. To be sure, sir. He's turned out a fiery rebel, after all—and a captain, to boot.

Els. Heaven bless me, but this is very sad. A promising youth to be led astray! Dear me, dear me! Rose, I am very sorry to say that this is certainly your fault. You have filled him with your wild, radical, and absurd heroic rhapsodies. You have made him disloyal to his king. You have put a dagger in his hand, to stab at the heart of his country. Alas! I see what the end will be—disgrace and death, ignominy and the gallows. [ROSE *walks back to the window.*

Kate. Mr. Metcalf, how are your little charges? How flourishes the birch?

Met. They've all caught the spirit of the rebellion, marm, and are as untractable as bulls. Bless you, there isn't a lad over fourteen who hasn't abandoned his horn-book and gone off with Armstrong. And as for the girls, they're greater rebels than the boys. What do you think, marm? The other day they came marching in procession, and demanded to know on which side I was. I said "God save the king;" whereupon they fell upon me like a swarm of bees, armed with a thousand pins, and so pinched, and pricked, and pulled me, that there wasn't a square inch of my skin that wasn't as full of holes as a ten-year old pin-cushion. And I do believe they never would have stopped if I hadn't cried, "Huzza for Washington!"

Els. I hope, sir, that you will not be compelled to follow the example of your scholars, and turn soldier.

Met. Never, sir. I content myself with teaching the young idea how to shoot, without indulging in such dangerous practices myself.

Rose. [*From the window,* R.] Why, there's Harry—father, Kate—Harry is dismounting at the door.

Els. Bless me! Is it possible? [*All gather around the window.*

Kate. It is, I declare—and how splendid he looks. Harry! Harry!

[*All salute him, and shake their handkerchiefs*

Met. [*Aside to* ROSE.] Hist! Miss Elsworth!

Rose. Eh!

Met. Walter is near—a note—

Rose. [*Seizing it, and reading hurriedly.*] "Will be with you to-day"——

Kate. [*Looking towards* R., *at the window.*] Doesn't he look fine! There's his step in the hall.

[*They all go towards door.* ROSE *conceals* WALTER's *note.*

Harry. [*Within.*] Rose, Kate, father!

Enter LIEUT. HARRY ELSWORTH, R. 1 E. *All gather around him with exclamations of welcome.*

Met. [*Aside.*] I'll take occasion to steal down stairs, and plague Bridget into a kiss or two. Delicious Bridget! [*Exit* METCALF, L. 1 E

Els. Harry! My brave lad!

Rose. Dear brother!

Harry. Dear sister! Father!

Els. Stand aside, girls. Let me have a look at him. Harry! Harry! You are a splendid-looking fellow, you are. Ha, ha, ha! Your hand, my boy. You look like a soldier, sir.

Harry. I have good news for you. I have just rode on before to acquaint you that Major Cleveland will honor your roof to-day.

Els. He shall be welcome—open doors and open hands.

Harry. He will remain until to-morrow. Now, girls, some of us young fellows are dying for a dance—can't we extemporize a ball?

Rose. Good gracious, Harry! You will have to pit coat against coat —where are your ladies?

Harry. Oh, we'd drum them up. There are a dozen families within as many miles.

Rose. A mad idea.

Harry. A wild one, I confess.

Els. It would be a suitable festivity in honor of our Long Island victory. Come girls, you have my consent.

Enter SERVANT, *announcing* CAPTAIN ARMSTRONG.

Enter CAPTAIN WALTER ARMSTRONG, R. 1 E.

All [*but* ROSE]. Captain Armstrong!

Arms. Captain Armstrong!

All [*but* ROSE]. In the continental service?

Arms. In the continental service!

Els. I am somewhat surprised, sir, at this visit. When you were a loyal gentleman my doors were always open to you—now, in that dress, I cannot consent to receive your visits. In happier moments you were a companion of my daughters—a friend of my son—you have selected a course which must terminate that connection with my family.

Arms. You will pardon me sir, I trust, for this intrusion. I have reached this place with some danger, for these parts abound with a set of fellows who have a fancy for wishing everybody else's skin the color of their own coats. Mr. Elsworth, my sense of duty has compelled me to pursue a path which has estranged me from your friendship. Let me ask frankly, sir, if it must separate me from one who has honored me with her consideration and affection?

Els. You allude to my daughter—to Rose——

Arms. I do, sir.

Els. *Mister* Armstrong—for I acknowledge no title bestowed by an unlawful authority—I would rather wed my daughter to a Turk than to one who had so forgotten his duty to his country.

[*Goes up.*—ARMSTRONG *bows.*

Harry. Walter, we were friends once, but, as his majesty's servant, I can offer no compromise to a rebel. *Now* you must not think of a union with our family. [*Goes up.*

Rose. This is nothing but blind prejudice. It has neither sense nor justice. Hear me. That for which you discard him places him higher in my esteem—shows me how worthy he is of the respect and honor of every true woman. My greatest pride is that he to whom I have pledged my hand wears those colors.

Arms. Generous girl!

Els. Rose, you pain me inexpressibly!

Rose I am not a giddy girl, sir. I'm a woman—old enough to know my own heart, and to decide between right and wrong. Walter, go, and carry with you assurances of my unwavering fidelity.

Enter BRIDGET, *hurriedly*, C.

Brid. Oh, my good gracious! dear me, good gracious! gracious, goodness, me! Such a lot of soldiers—all coming down the road.

Arms. Eh? Red or blue?

Brid. Bless me, goodness gracious, you here, Mr. Armstrong? You'd better look out, sir, for they are red coats, and there's a big number of them, too.

Arms. I must vanish. [*Running to the window*] Why, we're surrounded on every side. By Jove, I'm in a trap!

Rose. What will you do?

Arms. To the north of the house. Perhaps I can reach the forest——

Brid. They're all around that way, sir.

Harry. I wish that you could escape, Walter, without my knowledge. This is the regiment to which I belong. You were foolhardy to venture here.

Arms. I believe I'm caged, that's certain. And I've no desire to be caught either, for they bear especial malice against me. If they should know me for the fellow who played a certain trick upon them, an hour's time would suffice for them to make me an ornament to one of your old oaks on the lawn—a style of decoration that might suit their taste, but which wouldn't accord with my fancy.

Rose. Do they know your person?

Arms. From description, probably.

Rose. We must conceal you, then.

Arms. If you've a rat hole into which you can crowd me.

Harry. I must be ignorant of your movements. I will go and receive hem. [*Exit*, R. 1 L.

Arms. Whose command is it?

Rose. Major Cleveland's.

Arms. Eh? The man of men who itches to get hold of my insignificant person. He has offered £50 for it.

Kate. [*At the window.*] Away! They are dismounting at the door.

Rose. You, Bridget—I can trust you—quick to the loft with him.
Kate. [*Still at the window.*] Quick! quick!
Arms. Stow me away among your rubbish.

[ROSE *urges them off.* WALTER *snatches a kiss from* ROSE'S *hand as he exits with* BRIDGET, L. 1 E.

Kate. I do declare Captain Arbald is below, and I am sadly deranged.

Rose. Oh, fearfully! Run to your glass by all means. Set your springes, for these red birds are rare game.

Kate. Sister! But I'll be revenged. [*Exit* KATE, D. 2 E. R.

Enter MAJOR CLEVELAND, R. 1 E., *ushered in by* LIEUT. ELSWORTH, *who withdraws.*

Els. My dear Major Cleveland, let me welcome you zealously to this abode.

Cleve. A great many thanks, my dear Elsworth. I'm delighted to meet so true-hearted a loyalist. We pushed our march to partake of your hospitality. Ah, Miss Elsworth! How shall I express my delight in finding that Time, who deals so inexorably with us, has been induced to favor you. It gives me infinite pleasure, Miss Elsworth, to meet you once again, for the recollection of the occasions we have met previously, are bright spots in my memory.

Rose. Oh, sir, I thank you.

Els. And how, sir, comes on the royal cause? Will it be long ere these rebels are taught their duty to their king?

Cleve. Have no apprehensions, my dear Elsworth. Another campaign will scatter them to the mountains, and a live rebel be so great a curiosity, that to cage one and exhibit him would make a showman's fortune.

Rose. [*Aside.*] If he knew there were a caged one here now!

Els. But come, Major Cleveland, where are your companions? I must see why they have not followed you.

Cleve. They are delayed for a moment with the troop. By the way, Miss Elsworth, I believe that there are a couple of gentlemen without, who are old admirers of yours—Captain Arbald, and Lieutenant Marvin.

Rose. Old, Major! You flatter my taste.

Cleve. Why, with beauty I thought the conquest of the morning stale matter by night.

Rose. Oh, sir, if staleness went to make their age, they would be proverbed instead of Methuselah.

Cleve. They took very much to you.

Rose. So did the measles, sir.

Cleve. They are desperately enamored of you—would do any difficult thing—even die for you.

Rose. So they once told me, but I courtesied, and replied that I should prefer a live rebel to even two dead loyalists.

Cleve. And then——

Rose. They vowed to live for me. I begged of them to put themselves to no such inconvenience; that I wouldn't trouble them to do anything of the kind; that if they didn't think it worth while to live for themselves, I shouldn't intrude upon any suicidal intention they might entertain.

Cleve. And so they lived——

Rose. But I had no hand in it; I am innocent; my skirts are clear of the melancholy fact.

Cleve. They are noble gentlemen, Miss Elsworth. You must bear with me if I defend them. They are good soldiers, and fine-looking fellows.

Rose. For which I thank their tailors.

Cleve. Gay, dashing; brave of heart, and witty of tongue.

Rose. Then they have been studying the almanac. When I saw them last, they hadn't a grain of wit—not even by scratching.

Cleve. Really, Mr. Elsworth, your daughter has a sharp tongue.

Els. It is her humor, sir. Her passes are but play.

Cleve. I'll be sworn her heart is as true as her wit. She is——

Rose. Rebel, sir, from top to toe!

Enter ARBALD, MARVIN, *and* HARRY, R. 1 E.

Ah, gentlemen, my best welcome. My father will be proud to greet you——

Els. And most happy to know you, gentlemen.

Enter SERVANT, *with wine*, L.

Major Cleveland, will you do me the honor——

Cleve. Sir, I esteem it an honor. Gentlemen, I hope you will all fill in honor of our host. [*They gather around, fill, and drink to* MR. ELSWORTH, L.] Fill again, gentlemen, and honor the toast I am going to propose. The ladies! speedy priests and rings.

Rose. A doubtful compliment, Major Cleveland.

Cleve. Can you think so?

Rose. Ay, sir; for marriages, though called matches, are mostly sad patch-work.

Cleve. And the unmarried——

Rose. Oh, they are even worse. Old maids and old bachelors are the tossed about odds and ends of humanity.

Cleve. [*Going over to her.*] The happiest wit, madam, I ever heard.

Rose. Captain Arbald, will you grant me your arm? I'm sure you would like a turn in the garden. I shouldn't wonder if my sister were upon the grounds. Lieut. Marvin, will you go with us? Kate is dying for the sight of a red-coat. [*Exit*, C. D.

Cleve. A merry-hearted woman, Mr. Elsworth. There is a touch of sly deviltry in her composition.

Els. I fear lest her indiscreet tongue——

Cleve. Not at all, my dear friend! Lieutenant, I have been informed within an hour, that one Captain Armstrong has been seen this day within five miles of this place. On account of his connection with a certain affair, I wouldn't let him escape me at any sacrifice. I have already dispatched dragoons in his pursuit. At earliest dawn I shall expect you to head a detachment in his search. Meanwhile, sir, I should be grateful for an opportunity to repair my toilet.

Harry. This way, sir; I myself will conduct you to a chamber.

[*Exeunt* CLEVELAND *and* HARRY, D. 2 E. L.

Els. This is a situation indeed, for a royalist gentleman. My house filled with the king's officers, and a proscribed rebel concealed above. If discovered, I tremble to think of the consequences. [*Exit*, R. 1 E

Enter ROSE, C. D.

Rose. Thank Heaven; I am rid of them. Now to Walter, and learn his full danger.

Enter ARMSTRONG, L. 1 E.

Are you mad? What are you here for? Back to your hiding place at once.

Walter. No, Rose; I shall not go.

Rose. Why—what——

Walter. Hear me, Rose. Ask yourself if it is an honorable course for me, a proscribed and hunted rebel, to suffer myself to be concealed in your father's house when my discovery would involve him in terrible consequences. I cannot consent to expose him to those consequences. I would rather openly deliver myself into the hands of Major Cleveland.

Rose. Foolish man! You are ruining all. Walter, for my sake go back again. This is a ridiculous and false sense of honor

Walter. No, Rose, I am resolved——

Rose. Walter, I implore you——

Enter MAJOR CLEVELAND, 2 D. L.

[*Aside*.] Ha! Lost! [*Aloud*.] Oh, Major Cleveland, how opportune. Pray let me make you acquainted with Captain Fuller. A friend of my father's, sir—a neighbor. Captain Fuller, Major Cleveland. Allow me to commend you, gentlemen, to each other's better acquaintance.

Cleve. A rebel officer. This is very extraordinary.

Rose. Let me see you shake hands, gentlemen, for here, you know you must be friends. If you like to cut each other's throats elsewhere so be it; but, of course, you sheathe your swords, and swear peace in the presence of a lady.

Cleve. Miss Elsworth well rebukes us. Captain Fuller, for the time being, the red and the blue rejoice under a common auspices—Miss Elsworth smiles. [*They shake hands ceremoniously*.

Rose. Now, gentlemen, sit down. You, major, shall have a seat upon the sofa by my side. Captain Fuller, please, take the chair near you. [*The gentlemen seat themselves*.] Now, you see, I am between you, and shall prevent warfare. I here proclaim a truce. The captain major, wants to join our ball to-night. I have promised him my hand the next after yours.

Cleve. [*Scrutinizing* WALTER *closely*.] I'm quite ready, Miss Elsworth, to laugh at a joke, but really I cannot understand——

Rose. Why two gentlemen cannot meet under my father's roof, as his guests, and not fall to tearing each other to pieces? Is it the modern way to make war in parlors, instead of the field?

Cleve. Strange, very strange. Your pardon, Captain Fuller, but I cannot help remarking that you closely resemble a description I have received of one Captain Armstrong.

Rose. Dear me, and who is Captain Armstrong, pray?

Cleve. A rebel, madam.

Rose. I like him for that.

Cleve. A spy.

Rose. But what has all this to do with Captain Fuller? I have known the captain, major, for some years, and I think you can take my word for it, he is no spy.

Cleve. Do Captain Fuller and Captain Armstrong wear the same colors?

Walter. All continental officers wear the same colors.

Cleve. Are they all of the same complexion, height, and [*Rising and going over to him.*] do they all wear the same love tokens? Does Captain Fuller wear Captain Armstrong's sash, worked with Captain Armstrong's name!

Walter. [*Aside.*] The sash Rose worked and gave me. Fool! fool!

Cleve. Miss Elsworth, I'm under the necessity of a disagreeable duty. I am compelled to consider our truce at an end. Young sir, you are my prisoner.

Walter. [*Drawing and rushing between the Major and the door.*] If you speak aloud, or attempt to call aid, I will strike you dead. I shall not yield without resistance. If you molest me, blood will be shed.

Cleve. [*Drawing a pistol.*] I am better armed than you supposed, sir. It would be awkward for any collision to occur in the presence of a lady, and yet I shall not hesitate to do my duty. If you are really Captain Fuller, I shall be very glad to shake hands and drink a glass of wine with you; if Captain Armstrong, you *must* become my prisoner.

Rose. [*Standing by her chair, trembling.*] Gentlemen! Gentlemen!

Walter. I have but one reply to make: if you attempt to arrest me, I shall defend myself—and will escape if I can.

[*Several shots fired within.*

Enter MR. METCALF *suddenly*, C. D., *pursued by two soldiers.*

Cleve. Ha!

Met. (*Not seeing* CLEVELAND, *and rushing up to* WALTER.) Bless me, Captain Armstrong.

Cleve. Oh, then he is Captain Armstrong.

Rose. (*With great suddenness.*) Captain Fuller, Mr. Metcalf—don't play your jests here—Captain Fuller, sir.

Met. Eh! Eh! (*Looking confused from one to another.*) A jest, Captain Fuller—capital—ha, ha, ha—(*aside to* ROSE.) What mischief have I tumbled into now, and who is that fellow in a very red coat and a very white wig?

Rose. (*Aside to him.*) Major Cleveland.

Met. Major Cleveland! We are all hanged and quartered—though for the matter of that, in my capacity of expounder of the alphabet, I've been quartered—on the neighborhood, these ten years past. Your obedient servant, sir, your very obedient—

Cleve. That will do, fellow. What was the cause of those shots just now? (*To soldiers.*)

Met. 'Pon my word, sir, it was the guns.

Cleve. Pshaw!

Soldier. This fellow attempted to pass without the counter-sign.

Met. You see, sir, I was just about to enter to call on my friend, Mr. Elsworth, to sip an afternoon glass with him, when a big-booted fellow cried out, halt. Now, sir, the idea of asking a man well in both legs to halt, is preposterous. So I said, and walked on as straight as I could, when bang, bum, whiz, came one, two, three bullets scattering after my hide— (METCALF L.)

Cleve. Have done, sir. (*To* WALTER.) I am desirous of giving you, sir, every opportunity to disprove your identity with Captain Armstrong. I chance to know that gentleman's handwriting. There is a desk with pen and ink. Will you stand that test?

Wal. (*Aside to* ROSE.) That would never do. There isn't one of my pot-hooks that wouldn't hang me.

Rose. (*Quickly.*) Really, Major Cleveland, you might require a more reasonable test. Don't you see the captain has a rheumatic hand.

Cleve. For a rheumatic hand, Miss Elsworth, he handled his sword somewhat skilfully, just now. You see, sir, resistance is useless. You will resign your sword, I trust.

[*The two* SOLDIERS, *at a sign from* CLEVELAND, *have come up behind* WALTER. *He is seized.*]

Wal. Ha! I am your prisoner, sir.

Enter MR. ELSWORTH R. 1 E., *and* HARRY L. 2 E.

Els. What's this?

Cleve. I regret to say, my dear Elsworth, that this gentleman must, for a few hours, remain my prisoner. A mere form, sir. He will, doubtless, be free in a few days. I shall have to make use of one of your barns, sir. It is really a pity that the captain must be deprived of the dance to-night, but I will take care that his confinement shall not be severe.

Rose. This, sir, is a shameful breach of hospitality. Captain Armstrong is my father's guest, no less than yourself. Every consideration of delicacy and honor requires you to consider him so.

Cleve. Miss Elsworth, I could wish you not to consider me wrong or cruel in this.

Rose. I judge, sir, by what I see.

Cleve. You are severe.

Rose. I am glad you find me so.

Cleve. Will you not say peace?

Rose. War, Major Cleveland, to the last.

Els. Daughter, more courtesy.

Rose. Oh! father, they may chain and bind our poor country, but they cannot find a way to chain a free woman's free tongue.

Cleve. Lieutenant Elsworth, I place the Captain in your charge. Conduct him to a safe place.

Harry. This is the hard necessity of duty.

Els. And this will really be nothing serious?

Cleve. A bagatelle, I do assure you, sir.

Wal. (*Aside.*) I thank him for calming the fears of the family—but I know how hard it will go with me.

Harry. Walter—

Wal. I go, Harry. Rose!

Rose. (*Aside, with a sudden thought.*) Go! Say nothing.

Wal. Come, sir. (*To* HARRY.)

ROSE *assumes an air of cool indifference, and flings herself carelessly in a chair* E. MAJOR CLEVELAND (R.) *appears astonished.* MR. ELSWORTH *and the others look surprised and incredulous.*

PICTURE TO CLOSE OF ACT.

ACT II.

SCENE.—*A Garden—House in the background* L., *illuminated.*

Enter ROSE *and* MAJOR CLEVELAND *from house*, ROSE *hanging on the* MAJOR'S *arm.*

Rose. It was really absurd—was it not?—to think me the champion of that country clown. Poor fellow! I couldn't bear his discomfited looks, major, and so, out of old companionship, what could I do less than stand up for him? There won't be anything positively serious, will there, eh? I should be sorry to have it so, inasmuch as he fell into the trap under my father's roof. But don't you think I made a good champion? It was really presumptuous for the fellow to come here, though. These rustic clowns thrust themselves everywhere.

Cleve. What, Miss Elsworth, Captain Armstrong, then, is nothing—

Rose. Nothing in the world, I assure you, but a harmless country lad! Do tell me, major, am I not a good actor?

Cleve. Excellent. I really could have supposed that this American stood high in your esteem.

Rose. Oh, I like him, well enough. He is among the best the country affords, but that is very bad, you know.

Cleve. Then you bear me no malice?

Rose. Not enough to kill a gnat.

Cleve. Ah, Miss Elsworth, this assurance gives me the greatest pleasure.

Rose. Don't hurt the poor fellow though, major, I beg of you. I should be quite sorry if anything happened to him. He is a good-natured, useful neighbor enough—an unpolished jewel, papa calls him. Ah, major, our social wants in this community are lamentable enough, when we are obliged to content ourselves with such a poor substitute as you have seen, for all the polish and manner of London circles.

Cleve. Lamentable, indeed, Miss Elsworth.

Rose. The war brings one boon, at least,—the society of gentlemen.

Cleve. Very true, indeed.

Rose. [*Aside.*] Hem! Major Cleveland, I'll so wheedle you this night you shall cry enough to a woman, even if it so happen that you have never done it to a man. So look to it, my valiant major! Look to it!

Cleve. Do you know, dear Miss Elsworth, that I could wish to see you in these troubled times united to some one who could afford you the protection which only a husband can extend?

Rose. [*Behind her fan.*] Oh, major!

Cleve. [*Taking her hand.*] I cannot be mistaken in the surmise that you love already.

Rose. [*With a sigh.*] Oh, sir!

Cleve. Miss Elsworth! Rose! Confide in me! I am your friend.

Rose. [*With affected confusion.*] I believe you, Major Cleveland. I—I—really sir—I implore you to believe me—I have nothing to confide.

Cleve. Do not be offended, Miss Elsworth. I have your interest at heart. Pardon me—but Captain Arbald—[ROSE *starts and appears agitated,*] believes, or at least hopes, that he is acceptable to you. I am very deeply his friend—very deeply yours.

Rose. It is very pleasant to hear you say so, Major Cleveland.

Cleve. Then you do look upon him with favor?

Rose. Alas, Major Cleveland, these wars, these wars!

Cleve. They separate us from those who are dearest to us—they come between us and our hearts' affections.

Rose. Do they not daily threaten us with a heart widowhood?

Cleve. Ah, Miss Elsworth—Rose, let me call you—I see you are thinking of the young captain. You love him!

Rose. [*Aside.*] Walter, I must save you by whatever means! [*Aloud.*] Oh, major, let me beg of you one thing—let me hear you promise what I will ask you. You assure me you are my friend. Then grant me a pledge. Promise me to—to protect——

Cleve. The captain——

Rose. Who is to be my husband.

Cleve. You delight me. Are you then pledged?

Rose. We are.

Cleve. The young rascal. He never told me so. And jealous enough, I'll be sworn he is, to see me monopolize your society as I do.

Rose. His life is almost in your hands. Often you can save him from danger.

Cleve. You will marry him?

Rose. [*Abashed.*] Yes.

Cleve. I give you the pledge then, you ask. Make him your husband, and for your sake I will defend and protect him to the extent of my power.

Rose. Oh, sir, you make me happy. I am, major, a foolish girl. I place, perhaps, absurdly, so much confidence in your ability to rescue him from many dangers—that I should like—should like, sir, to wear this ring [*Slipping one from his finger.*] as a friendly pledge that you will be his guardian, his watchful protector.

Cleve. Let me kiss the ring upon your finger as a formal seal to my pledge.

Rose. It becomes an oath now.

Cleve. It does—sworn upon this hand.

Rose. That you are his friend—ever to be my husband's friend.

Cleve. That is the oath. I take it again!

Rose. [*Aside.*] Now, Major Cleveland, I have you!

Cleve. [*Aside.*] She shall be his—then—why then to make her mine.

Rose. [*Aside.*] There is some libertine scheme behind all this, I feel assured. He is playing the villain. Well, well! Shall we go in?

Enter ARBALD, L. 2 E.

Cleve. Ah, Arbald. We have been looking for you.

Rose. I believe, captain, that I am pledged to you for the next dance.

Arbald. It is my happiness to recollect it. But one dance is missed.

Rose. Let me make amends.

Enter MARVIN, *hurriedly*, E. 1 E.

Marvin. Sir, the rebel has escaped.

Cleve. Ha! What do you mean? How?

Marvin. It is uncertain how.

Cleve. He must be about the grounds somewhere. Put your fellows upon his track. Hunt him out! I wouldn't lose my hold upon him for the value of a dozen ordinary rebels. [*Crosses*, L.

[*During this speech* ARMSTRONG, R. 3 E., *glides in behind among the shrubbery and touches* ROSE. ROSE *starts, and slightly screams. All turn quickly toward her. She, hastily and unseen, unclasps a bracelet from her arm, and flings it behind her.*]

Rose. Gentlemen! gentlemen! gentlemen! I've lost my bracelet—a valued bracelet. Five minutes ago I had it on my arm. Major Cleveland—Captain Arbald—I beseech you to search for it. What could have become of it?

Cleve. (L. C.) Your bracelet?

Rose. Gentlemen, I implore you to search for it. Major, it may have been dropped in the bower. Go look for it, sir. Captain Arbald and Lieutenant Marvin, why do you stand idly there? Do you refuse to search for my jewel? I've lost a bracelet, I tell you, sirs. Is this the way you attend upon the wishes of a lady?

Cleve. Really, Miss Elsworth, duty——

Rose. Don't talk to me of duty, sir. I would not lose my bracelet for the wealth of the world. A valued token from a dear friend; I swore never to part with it. Oh, indeed, you are gallant gentlemen! You let me lose a precious jewel, and you stand staring by. I tell you, I value that bracelet with my very life.

Cleve. But the escaped prisoner?

Rose [*Passionately.*] What is the prisoner to me? What is he to my bracelet? Must I lose my bracelet for the sake of a runaway rebel—a miserable clown, who may either hang or run, I care not? Some one will tread upon my bracelet, [*walking up and down impetuously,*] one of the common soldiers will find and keep it. I would not lose it for worlds.

Arbald. Indeed, Miss Rose, I assure you—— [L. *of* CLEVELAND.

Rose. Oh, no assurances, sir. Where is your devotion to me? Where your willingness to sacrifice everything for me, as I have heard you swear more than once? If you ever expect to come into my presence again, you must first clasp that bracelet on my arm. I will hear nothing, listen to no excuse; and if you refuse to obey me, never let me see you again.

Cleve. [*Aside.*] I must not lose my hold upon her, by offending her. [*Aloud.*] Gentlemen, do you remain with Miss Elsworth, and search for the lost jewel. I will myself give the necessary order for the search for the missing prisoner. [*Exit* CLEVELAND, L. 1 E

Rose. You, captain, search yonder bower.

Arbald. Were you there?

Rose. Or I should not send you. [*Exit* ARBALD, R. 3 E.] Marvin, go hunt the rooms—I cannot say what moment I dropped it.

Marvin. I obey Miss Elsworth. [*Exit* MARVIN, L. 2 E

Rose. Where can he be—if my *ruse* has only given him time.

Enter WALTER, *hurriedly*, R. 2 E.

Good heavens! Not off! Here yet!

Walter. Every outlet is guarded: could I reach the house——

Rose. This way—we may steal in——

Wal. I found your jewel, Rose!

[*As they are hurrying off, Enter* MAJOR CLEVELAND, L. 1 E.

Caught, as I'm alive!

Rose. Quick! away——

Wal. It shall be so—— [*Rushes off in an opposite direction*, R. 1 E.

Cleve. Ha! ho! Guard! Corporal!

Enter CORPORAL *and* GUARD *rapidly, with torches.*

That way is your prisoner. Find him, I charge you.

[*Exeunt* CORPORAL *and* GUARD, R. 1 E.

What am I to think, Miss Elsworth?

Rose [*Vehemently.*] Think! That I would give the world for Captain Armstrong to escape.

Cleve. Humph! The gift would be useless. Look for yourself.

Rose. [*Looking off, then suddenly burying her face in her hands.*] Good Heavens!

Cleve. [*In her ear.*] How's this, Miss Elsworth? [*She starts up, proudly.*]

Enter SOLDIERS, *guarding* WALTER, R. 1 E.

I rejoice, sir, that we meet again.

Soldier. A jewel, sir, found upon the prisoner.

Cleve. Ha! what's this? [*Reading the inscription by a torch.*] "To Rose, from Walter!" Madam, I understand you now. I was deceived. Permit me to be the means of restoring this valued token from a dear friend. Would it not be a strange vicissitude if the finding of the trinket should be the means of losing the friend? Conduct your prisoner hence. [*Exeunt all but* ROSE *and* CLEVELAND, R. 3 E.

Rose. Major Cleveland, Captain Armstrong must be allowed to go free. I have your promise. I hold you to it.

Cleve. My promise——

Rose. Look! [*Pointing to the signet received from the Major.*]

Cleve. Aha! Then it was Captain Armstrong, and not Captain Arbald, to whom you alluded in our interview. I was beginning to suspect the trick.

Rose. Your shrewdness would have done you more credit if you had detected it before. As it is, I have your signet and your promise to save Captain Armstrong.

Cleve. But the promise referred only to your husband.

Rose. Captain Armstrong is my betrothed husband.

Cleve. Ay, but at present is a prisoner. You see, madam, I hold the cards.

Rose. Your pardon, sir, but I have the game.

Cleve. Eh! Is not the captain in my hands?

Rose. Before to-morrow morning he shall be in mine.

Cleve. Confound it, madam, I'll keep so strict a guard upon him, a fly shan't light upon him without my knowing it.

Rose. Do so, and if you were argus-eyed into the bargain, I'd marry him before to-morrow morning.

Cleve. Ha! is it come to that? I'll march this hour.

Rose. It would be too late.

Cleve. This moment, then.

Rose. I would anticipate you.

Cleve. Zounds, madam, you talk idly.
Rose. Zounds, sir, you talk without reason.
Cleve. I'll go to him at once—put a pistol to his head—blow his brains out, and——
Rose. Make me his widow.
Cleve. Deuce take it, you're mad.
Rose. Mad if you will, Major Cleveland. It is a struggle between us. Look to it, sir. You may be bold, valorous, cunning—vastly so; but you have a woman's wit against you—so look to it!
Cleve. Confound it.
Rose. Bravo! bravo! Your passion, sir, well becomes you——
Cleve. Deaths and devils! *Exit* R. 1 E.
Rose. Ha, ha, ha!

Enter METCALF, L. 1 E.

Here! Here, Mr. Metcalf—follow Major Cleveland; watch every step; don't lose sight of him for a moment.
Met. Trust me; I'll be his shadow from this time forth.
Exeunt separately.

Enter CAPTAIN ARBALD *and* KATE, R. 3 E.

Arb. Really, Miss Kate, you do me injustice—but if I could only induce you to intercede——
Kate. Plead your cause for you. [*Aside.*] Blind and stupid! Can't he see that I am dying for that my sister laughs at.
Arb. If I could but find that lost bracelet——
Kate. Hush! Who comes here? [*They withdraw.*

Enter MAJOR CLEVELAND, MR. ELSWORTH, LIEUTENANT ELSWORTH, *and* METCALF *behind.*

Mr. E. Declared to you that she would marry Captain Armstrong—
Cleve. Yes, my dear sir, and I felt it my duty to acquaint you.
Harry. I will go to the captain and demand a satisfactory——
Cleve. Your pardon, young gentleman. Captain Armstrong is now my prisoner; and I shall hold him safe for my own purposes.
Mr. Els. In face of my commands this day pronounced. It is monstrous. I must seek out Rose, and have an explanation. [*Exit* R. 1 E.]
Kate. [*Aside to* ARBALD.] You see, sir, how little the bracelet would plead in your cause.
Arb. I do, indeed. [*They saunter off.*
Harry. (R.) I do not, sir, often ask favors of you. This day my father forbade Armstrong from entertaining any intentions relative to my sister. He has insulted me, my father, and Rose. I wish to chastise him, sir.
Cleve. (L.) Tut, tut! I will not give his cunning a chance to plan another escape. The best thing you can do is to help me to prevent the possibility of the marriage.
Harry. You are my superior. I have no choice but to obey. But I long to inflict the punishment due to his treachery. [*Exit.*
Cleve. Pest on't, I love the wench. I thought, if married to Arbald, and frequently near me, my suit might flourish. But the cunning vixen caught me in my own trap. If I could only trip her now; let me see—let me see.

Enter ARBALD.

Cleve. Ah, Arbald, come hither. How flourishes your suit with Miss Elsworth?

Arbald. Badly, I must confess.

Cleve. Unless we prevent it she will be married to this Armstrong before morning.

Arbald. Is it possible?

Cleve. I have my own reasons for desiring to break up the match between them—to prevent their marriage. Nothing occurs to me at all feasible to that end, but some plan to get introduced into Armstrong's presence a woman disguised as Rose.

Arbald. And marry them?

Cleve. Ay. Armstrong is on the alert for some scheme to rescue him—would fall into such a net as fishes do—and think it was his mistress' cunning to serve him.

Arbald. But where is the woman?

Cleve. Rose has a girl in attendance upon her who is near her size and figure—a mischievous wench, or I am no judge of physiognomies.

METCALF, *who has been listening aside,* Oho! [*Exits hurriedly and secretly.*]

Arbald. Bridget, they call her.

Cleve. Send her to me. Fifty pounds will be more than her fidelity can stand. Luckily we have the chaplain with us. Have him ready.

Arbald. I'll hunt Bridget up at once. [*Exit* ARBALD.

Cleve. The plan is a good one. Now, Lady Wit, those who win may laugh. But I was a blind fool ever to allow her to obtain that promise from me.

Enter METCALF, R. 1 E.

Met. Hist! Major Cleveland.

Cleve. Well, good follow.

Met. [*Aside.*] Fellow! It is remarkable now that I who daily make a score of urchins tremble in their shoes at the frown of my portentous brow, can't in the least make these people afraid of me. Let me see what effect one of my frightfully severe looks would have.

[*Walks up to him.*

Cleve. Well, sir, have you any business with me?

Met. No, no, sir. [*Aside.*] I suppose my urchins feel as I do now. [*Aloud.*] I've got an idea, sir, about the captain.

Cleve. Well, what idea?

Met. [*Aside.*] Here comes Rose—the very image of Bridget—all I wanted was to give her time. [*Aloud*] An idea—— [*Aside*] to trap you with sword, coat, and all——

Cleve. There she is—begone fellow—you intrude upon me.

Enter ROSE, *disguised as* BRIDGET, C. U. E. R.

Rose. [*Curtseying.*] Your Honor sent for me.

Met. Ha! ha! ha! Trap to catch foxes—ho! ho! ho! [*Exit,* R.

Cleve. You look a lively, quick-witted lass.

Rose. [*Aside.*] Now for the airs of your true lady's lady.

Cleve. Do you know how to keep a silent tongue?

Rose. Bless us! Haven't I always been in practice? Ain't I mum to what all the fine gentlemen say about the bouquets, the presents the love notes—

Cleve. How would you like to make twenty pounds?

Rose. Oh, sir, I am quite invincible.

Cleve. But twenty pounds?

Rose. Say twenty-five.

Cleve. To be paid when the contract is performed. How would you like to marry?

Rose. Oh! good gracions!

Cleve. Hush! Why the deuce do you raise that clatter?

Rose. Lor, sir, we always do.

Cleve. Be silent, or the twenty pounds——

Rose. Twenty-five——

Cleve. Twenty-five then. Marriage in jest.

Rose. Oh!

Cleve. Only in jest—to decide a wager. You must disguise yourself as your mistress, when you will be admitted into the presence of Captain Armstrong.

Rose. Captain Armstrong—Goodness gracious!

Cleve. Hear me out. A pretended chaplain will be by, and a sham form of marriage will be gone through with—

Rose. Only in jest? Why what a funny joke!

Cleve. Capital! capital! Ha! ha! ha!

Rose. Ha! ha! ha! A splendid joke, sir. But I don't quite understand it.

Cleve. Oh, you understand enough. You must not speak above the lowest whisper, nor let the captain see your features. A few words and the—the—ha, ha, ha--the joke is through with—

Rose. I see—I see.

Cleve. And then to-morrow when he comes to know it—don't you see—we will have a run on the captain—'twill be the rarest sport when found out.

Rose. But suppose now it should turn out to be a real no-mistake marriage.

Cleve. But it can't. The priest is a sham—that's the point of the joke.

Rose. That's the point of the joke, eh?

Cleve. Come, will you do it?

Rose. Well—I am doubtful.

Cleve. Only carry it out well, and you shall have fifty pounds.

Rose. I am convinced, as old intrigues are dull, I want pastime, and would like to earn fifty pounds, and if my chance in other quarters are uninjured, why——

Cleve. You will do it.

Rose. Will the captain think it a jest?

Cleve. He thinks there is a plan on foot to introduce your mistress to him for a similar purpose.

Rose. And when he finds that he has married plain Bridget instead of Miss Rose—what a rage he will be in! Oh, what a delightful jest—

Cleve. The funniest you ever heard of. Such laughing as there will be!

Rose. Fifty pounds—all in gold—is more than I can stand.

Cleve. Then meet me in five minutes, by yonder tree.

Rose. I'll slip on one of my mistress's dresses, and in five minutes be ready—but remember—*fifty pounds!* [*Exit* ROSE, R. 2 E.

Cleve. [*Rubbing his hands.*] The best of tricks. Ha! ha! ha! [*Exit* R.

Enter METCALF *and* ELSWORTH, R. 1 E.

Els. Ha, ha, ha! Bravo, Metcalf! a good jest, sir—Bridget disguised as Rose—ha! ha! ha!

Met. It's exquisitely funny, sir—only I think you don't quite understand it—

Els. It's you, Metcalf, that don't understand it. It's nothing but a piece of military deviltry. Why, my innocent sir, Armstrong's confinement is only a sham—it doesn't mean anything—Cleveland told me so himself—he will be free to-night. I shouldn't wonder if they were drinking and carousing together now. Bless you, Metcalf, it's only one of Cleveland's practical jokes. But I must go and find Rose, and tell her all about it—it will give her such a laugh. How the captain will stare when he finds it out, to be sure! [*Exit* L.

Met. Well, wise one, if you insist upon having it in that way, why do so—I suppose Miss Rose can fight her battles without your help. It was devilish lucky, though, I overheard that plan of theirs, or the captain would have been victimized—damnably—ay, damnably—if it be swearing—and a capital crime at Fidlington School. I wonder where Bridget is—Bridget *bona fide*—I mean—a de[illegible]ious girl,—I love her—I will conjugate her. Nobody in the walks—the marriage not over yet—bless me! I do believe that I am trembling like a refractory scholar with a prospective birching. If it should fail—but it won't, it can't—Rose is a girl to carry anything through.

Re-enter MR. ELSWORTH, L.

Els. Where can Rose be, I wonder! I can't find her anywhere. Everybody inquiring for her—everybody laughing too about the jest upon Armstrong. Ah, these military fellows are such practical jokers so full of deviltry to be sure! Who could have thought of such a trick?

Met. No civilian, you may be sure, sir. [*Aside, looking off.*] Eh? There they are. The deed is done. It's all right, ha! ha! ha! I'll cut. That major has a sanguinary way of contemplating me that has blood in it—blood! [*Aloud.*] I think I saw Rose in this direction, sir, with the major I dare say we can find her, if we go along.

Els. Come, sir, then. [*Exeunt,* L. 3 E.

Enter MAJOR CLEVELAND, R. 2 E.

Cleve. It's done, and they are fast married. Aha, my lady, who now has the game? Armstrong looked astounded, but expecting some plan to aid him, he fell into the trap without asking a question. Now now, my course is clear!

Enter ELSWORTH.

Els. Where can Rose be, to be sure? The guests are leaving, and I must find her to give them a good-night. Ah, Major! Have you seen my daughter?

Enter LIEUTENANT ELSWORTH.

Lieut. Els. Sir, sir, do you not know that Rose has clandestinely been introduced into the presence of Armstrong—

Els. No! has she, though? You d-o-n-t say so! Let me whisper a word, Master Harry—a beautiful joke—it was Bridget—

Lieut. Els. No sir, it was Rose herself.

Cleve. The young man is right.

Els. How! What do you say?

Cleve. Simply, sir, by the richest scheme in the world, this rebel's union with your daughter is rendered impossible. I told you the marriage was a jest—a sham. It was not—quite the contrary.

Els. Do I understand you to say, sir, that you have really tricked Captain Armstrong into a marriage with——

Cleve. To be sure, sir. It will be the sport of the whole army. The disgrace you feared cannot now occur. Miss Elsworth can never be that rustic's wife—thanks, sir, to my splendid idea. Aha, it was a glorious thought, glorious!

Els. Now, damn all respect for the red-coats.

Cleve. Ha!

Els. Sir, you have been guilty of a vile scheme. You have put my house to a dishonorable use. You have betrayed one of my guests infamously. Oh! that one of His Majesty's officers could lend himself to a scheme like this.

Cleve. Why, sir, I thought——

Enter ROSE *and* WALTER, *back.*

Els. That I would sanction such a plot. Major Cleveland, your conduct has made me half a rebel. It was devilish—diabolical, sir!

Cleve. But——

Enter METCALF, *dancing,* R. U. E.

Met. Armstrong has escaped.

Cleve. Escaped! Again! Impossible!

Met. He has, or may I be birched.

Enter LIEUT. MARVIN, L. 1 E.

Mar. Sir, the prisoner has escaped—and the woman——

Cleve. By Heaven! it shall not be—a hundred pounds reward for him!

Rose. [*Approaching with* WALTER.] I claim the reward, Major Cleveland.

Cleve. You! The prisoner here! How came he free?

Rose. By your signet. The sentry knew and acknowledged it.

Cleve. Miss Elsworth?

Rose. Mrs. Armstrong, by your kind assistance.

Cleve. Ha! What do you mean?

Rose. Permit me to present you to my husband.

Cleve. Your husband! What does this mean?

Rose. I *did have* the trump card, sir, and have taken the trick.

Cleve. I am bewildered—I cannot understand——

Rose. Can't you see? [*Imitating him.*] "How would you like to make twenty pounds? Ha, ha, ha! only as jest! a splendid jest! we'll have such a run on the captain! As I want pastime, and my prospects——

Cleve. The wench has betrayed me.

Rose. You never spoke a word to Bridget. I was the only person you saw.

Cleve. You!

Rose. Even I. Did I act it to the life?

Cleve. Caught! Tricked! Fool! By ——! Madam, this is a farce.

Rose. Sir, I know it, but it has been played out, and you unwittingly have acted the clown.

Els. I am confounded.

Cleve. The end is not yet. I refuse to be governed by a forced construction to a promise which I meant to apply differently. The rebel is still my prisoner. He is surrounded.

Rose. If your promise is not observed to the letter, I'll proclaim you through the army. I'll degrade you in the eyes of every English officer and gentleman in the land, You disgrace your sword, sir, by this very hesitation. Your bitter, unsoldierly, and dishonorable hatred and persecution of an honorable prisoner, drove me to an extremity which nothing but a question of life or death could have persuaded me to undertake. My womanly modesty I was forced to outrage. You compelled me to stoop to things which I abhorred. But I have a brother who is an English officer; a husband who is an American one. Be careful, sir, in what way you use my name in connection with this night's work, for, be assured, they will not fail to punish a ribald, a slanderous, or a libertine tongue. Consent to Captain Armstrong's release, and your discomfiture remains a secret; refuse, and with one word, I'll have all our guests upon the spot and a public confession.

Cleve. It's absurd to suppose that I'm to be bound by such figments as you have woven. The thing is too ridiculous.

Rose. You acknowledged the binding nature of your promise, when you attempted, with such heartless cruelty, to entrap the captain into a marriage with a servant. How would that story sound, think you? And what would be said of the sagacity and discernment of an officer who could allow such a deceit to be practised upon him as I practised upon you? Dear me! I think, major, that you are in a quandary.

Met. [L. *Aside*] In a ditch!

Rose. We await your decision. Shall the captain be free and this little jest go no further?

Cleve. Miss Elsworth——

Rose. Excuse me if I assist your memory—Mrs. Armstrong.

Cleve. Madam, I yield to a woman. You fight with weapons I d not understand——

Rose. With wit, eh?

Cleve. [*Aside.*] There is no hope for me. She has me at every point. I may as well yield with what grace I can. [*Aloud.*] Miss Elsworth, I am at your mercy. May not this night's work be forgotten? Captain Armstrong, I swore if ever I caught you, that you should pay dearly for that daring trick of yours—that bold capture of a fellow-officer, sleeping by my very side—but this lady has checkmated me.

Wal. Checkmated you, sir, and mated me.

Cleve. Both were done by the same move.

Els. (L. U. E.) And you are married, Rose?

Rose. (C.) I will bear Walter's name when we are publicly married, sir—which now, I trust, will be with your sanction.

Els. You have it. You have won a husband, if ever woman did.

Lieut. Els. Walter, if you were only more true to the right———

Arms. Oh, Harry! We will discuss that question yet. I shall make you [*In his ear.*] a convert; be sure of it.

Enter CAPTAIN ARBALD *and* KATE, L. U. E.

Kate. Why the company is breaking up. We missed you all, sadly. Here come the guests.

Cleve. Ah, Arbald, I'm afraid you will have to forego Miss Rose, here—

Arb. To pluck a flower no less sweet.

Rose. What? Why Kate———

Arb. I have your sister's consent, Miss Elsworth, conditioned only that you all accord with her decision.

Rose. And so you have been making love under the *rose* all this while. Do not doubt our good wishes.

Met. I wonder where Bridget is. I'll pop the question before morning.

Els. Rose, you have neglected your friends. Let us go in.

Rose. Our first duty is to the friends before us——

Arms. To which faction do they adhere—red or blue?

Rose. True blue and rebel, I'll be sworn—but I will ask them! [*Comes forward. To* ARMSTRONG.] You see, sir, they respond already. [*To the Audience.*] Do you approve the whiggish maid, and sanction her schemes so boldly played? The heart of love is heroic in every age; and after all

What difference can we affix,
'Twixt love to-day, and Love in '76?

KATE. ARBALD. ARMSTRONG. ROSE. ELSWORTH. CLEVELAND.

LIEUT. ELSWORTH. METCALF

CURTAIN.

THE END.

FRENCH'S SCENES FOR AMATEURS.

From approved designs. Representing scenes suitable for any piece. These are invaluable to amateur scene painters and also a great guide and help to professionals. Measurement 16½ in. by 12½ in.
Price Colored, each, 30 cents. Plain, each, 15 cents.

BACK SCENES.

The letters denote what borders and sides will go with the scenes.

1. Cottage, Interior (*j b*)	10. Library (*j*)	18. Attic (*b j*)
2. " Exterior (*a f*)	11. Street, Foreign (*e*)	19. Lodging House Room (*j*)
3. Wood (*a j*)	12. Roadside Inn with river and bridge (*k*)	20. Villa (*a f*)
4. Prison (*c l*)		21. Court of Justice (*h*)
5. Field (*a k*)	13. Foreign Hotel ext. (*af*)	22. Baronial Hall (*h b*)
6. Castle (*k*)	14. Ship Deck	23. Proscenium, right
7. Street (*g*)	15. Seascape (*k*)	23A " left
8. Palace (*d h*)	16. Cave (*c l*)	24. Curtain
9. Drawing-room (*j*)	17. Mountain Pass (*b k*)	25. Drop Scene.

BORDERS AND SIDES.

Price Colored, each, 30 cents Plain, each, 15 cents.

a Foliage Borders.	*e* Foreign Exterior Sides.	*j* Interior Sides.
b Rocks and Raft Borders.	*f* Tree Sides.	*k* Field and Rock Sides.
c Stone Borders.	*g* Exterior Sides.	*l* Stone Sides.
d Fancy Borders.	*h* Pillar Sides.	

FRENCH'S AMATEUR OPERAS,

FOR STAGE AND DRAWING-ROOM.

Comprising some of the best works of the great composers, and arranged so that they can be performed in any drawing-room. Each book is complete in itself, containing the *Libretto, Stage Directions, Music, Costumes, and Properties,* elegantly finished, and the size of ordinary music, illuminated cover.
This series is superior to any other published. The following are ready:

PRICE 40 CENTS EACH.	M	F
The Rose of Auvergne, or "Spoiling the Broth," 1 act. Music by Offenbach	2	1
The Blind Beggars, by Offenbach, 1 act	2	1
The Barber of Bath, Offenbach, 1 act	3	1
My New Maid, composed by Charles Lecocq, 1 act	0	2
A Fit of the Blues, composed by V. Robillard, 1 act	1	1
Grass Widows, V. Gabriel, 1 act	1	2
Loan of a Lover	4	2
Trial by Jury, composed by Arthur Sullivan, 1 act, words by W. S. Gilbert. This is very amusing and very pretty. There are five males, as well as twelve jurymen (the chorus), and one female character and eight bridesmaids, also the chorus. If these numbers be not convenient, any number will do	17	9

TABLEAUX VIVANTS,

ARRANGED FOR PRIVATE REPRESENTATION.

By J. V. PRICHARD.

Containing 80 selected Tableaux, with instructions how to get them up, cast of characters, costumes required, and full description of each picture. Also information respecting the use of the Tableaux Lights, and other effects, and describing the music required for each representation. Price, 25 cents.

THEATRICAL AND FANCY COSTUME WIGS, &c.,

A large assortment of above kept in Stock. No Wigs lent out on hire. Any Wig can be made to order. For prices and description, see

CATALOGUE, POST FREE ON APPLICATION.

S. FRENCH & SON,

38 East 14th Street, Union Square, New York.

FRENCH'S ACTING EDITIONS,

PRICE, 15cts. EACH.

NEW PLAYS
PUBLISHED IN FRENCH'S STANDARD DRAMA.

Lancers
Lucille
Randall's Thumb
Wicked World
Two Orphans
Colleen Bawn
'Twixt Axe and Crown
Lady Clancarty
Never Too Late to Mend
Lily of France
Led Astray
Henry V., new version
Unequal Match
May, or Dolly's Delusion
Allatoona
Enoch Arden
Weak Woman
How She Loves Him
Our Society
Mother in Law
Snowed In

NEW PLAYS
PUBLISHED IN FRENCH'S MINOR DRAMA.

Wonderful Woman
Curious Case
Forty Winks
As Like as Two Peas
Court Cards
Happy Land
Terrible Tinker
My Uncle's Will

NEW PLAYS
PUBLISHED IN FRENCH'S LONDON EDITION.

Twenty Minutes Under an Umbrella
Mr. Joffin's Latch Key
Watch and Wait
Family Pictures
Fatal Glass
Ashore and Afloat
Jeannette and Jeannot
Bridal Wreath
Gold Fiend
Tom Bowline
Narcisse, the Vagrant
The Vampire
Headless Horseman
Our Geordie
For Honor's Sake
Our Bitterest Foe
By Royal Command
Blow in the Dark
Painless Dentistry
Taking the Veil
Rely on My Discretion
Who Stole the Clock
Love and Honor
On the Clyde
Mary's Dream
Fame
Bitter Reckoning
Eileen Oge
Bathing
An Old Score
My Sister from India
Maria Martin
Among the Relics
Nabob for an Hour
An Old Man
Village Nightingale
Our Nelly
Partners for Life
Chopstick and Spikins
Chiselling
Birds in their Little Nests
Pretty Predicament
Seven Sins
Insured at Lloyd's
Hand and Glove
Keep Your Eye on Her
Jessamy's Courtship
False Alarm
Up in the World
Parted
One in Hand, &c.
Little Sunshine
Who'll Lend me a Wife
Extremes Meet
Golden Plough
Sweethearts
Velvet and Rags
Cut for Partner
Love's Alarms
An Appeal to the Feelings
Tale of a Comet
Under False Colors
Heroes
Philanthropy
Little Vixens
The Coming Woman
Telephone
Too Late to Save
Just My Luck
Grateful Father
Happy Medium
Sole Survivor
Neck or Nothing
Poppleton's Predicaments
Auld Acquaintance
Weeds
White Pilgrim
Dentist's Clerk

ARTICLES NEEDED BY AMATEURS,

Such as Tableaux Lights, Magnesium Tableaux Lights, Prepared Burnt Cork, Grease, Paints, Lightning for Private Theatricals.

Jarley's Wax Works, Ethiopian Plays, Charades, Amateur's Guide, Guide to the Stage.

NEW CATALOGUE SENT FREE.

S. FRENCH & SON,

38 E. 14th Street, Union Square, N. Y.

www.ingramcontent.com/pod-product-compliance
Lightning Source LLC
LaVergne TN
LVHW011138110826
845150LV00008B/2399
9781418193058